For Dimdigibuu ("Like a wolf"), my tsiits. She gave me
her patience, her confidence, and her love for our culture.
Her name now lives on with my aunt.

— H.G. / B.D.H.

For my brothers, Jesse and Riley, with love.
— N.D.

The Wolf Mother

By Hetxw'ms Gyetxw (Brett D. Huson)
Illustrated by Natasha Donovan

HIGHWATER
PRESS

In Bloom

Lasa 'yanja, the Budding Trees and Blooming Flowers Moon, is upon us. During this lunar cycle[1] in May, spring takes hold of the land, and the plants prepare for the summer to come. The air changes as the sun's warmth moves the spring currents, stirring up the scent of new blossoms. Lasa 'yanja is the season when many species[2] bring new life into the world. Nox Gibuu, the wolf mother, gave birth to six new wolf pups[3] only three short weeks ago.

[1] The **lunar cycle** refers to the moon's orbit around the earth.
[2] A **species** is a group of similar individuals that can reproduce.
[3] A **pup** is a baby wolf.

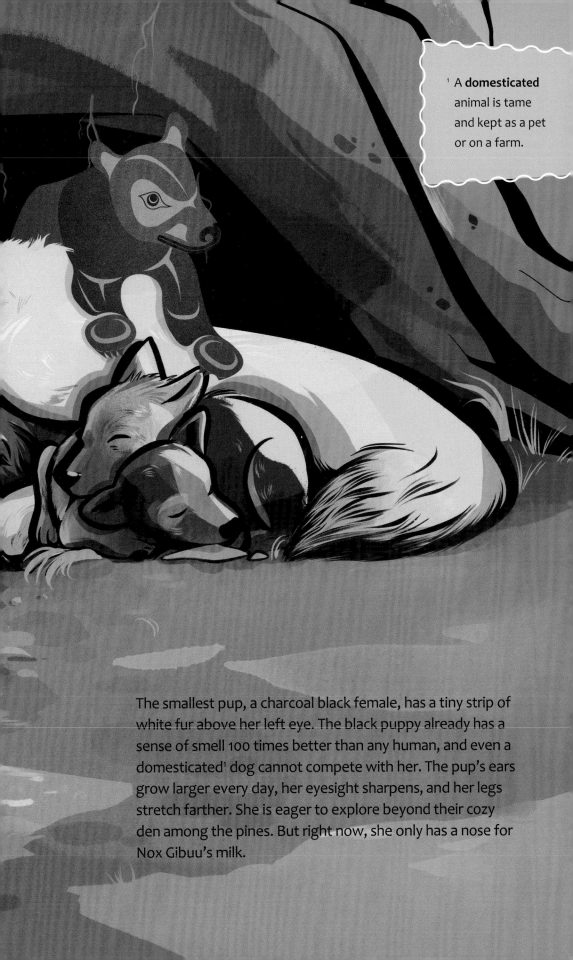

The smallest pup, a charcoal black female, has a tiny strip of white fur above her left eye. The black puppy already has a sense of smell 100 times better than any human, and even a domesticated¹ dog cannot compete with her. The pup's ears grow larger every day, her eyesight sharpens, and her legs stretch farther. She is eager to explore beyond their cozy den among the pines. But right now, she only has a nose for Nox Gibuu's milk.

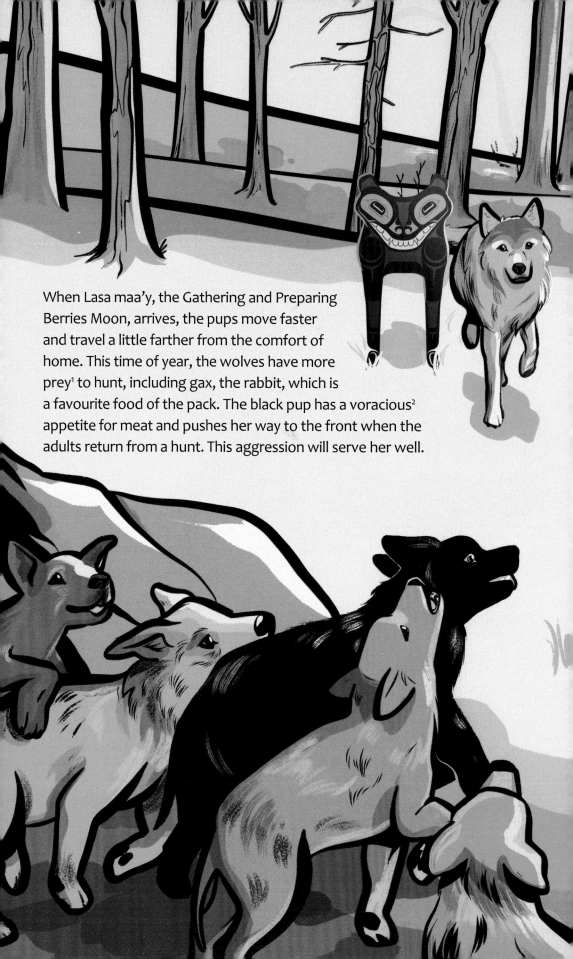

When Lasa maa'y, the Gathering and Preparing Berries Moon, arrives, the pups move faster and travel a little farther from the comfort of home. This time of year, the wolves have more prey[1] to hunt, including gax, the rabbit, which is a favourite food of the pack. The black pup has a voracious[2] appetite for meat and pushes her way to the front when the adults return from a hunt. This aggression will serve her well.

¹ **Prey** are animals that are hunted or killed by other animals for food.
² **Voracious** means having a huge appetite.

Disperse

After two years of growing, hunting, and running with her natal pack,[1] the black wolf feels a need to leave home. Physical changes urge her to seek out a group of her own. She is ready to become Nox Gibuu, the wolf mother.

It is the time of Lasa gangwiikw, the Groundhog Hunting Moon. The air is cold, and the groundhogs are cumbersome, fattened by their summer feeding. This time of year is perfect for this powerful wolf to venture out alone. Prey is plentiful[2] across their territory, and she will find lots to eat during her lonely trek.

Some weeks have passed, and Lasa gwineekxw, the Getting-Used-to-Cold Moon, is approaching. On this chilly November day, the sun breaks through the thick clouds that hang over the mountains. Yuukhl maadim, the snow is falling, and the rays of light reaching the forest floor set the scene about to unfold.

Silent as a light breeze, the black wolf glides across the terrain¹ with her piercing bright eyes locked on a small group of wolves. She has followed them for days, and two of them have come to welcome her and know her scent. A grey female in the group is wary of the black wolf's presence. Ears folded back, tail down low, the black wolf approaches the grey female, showing her teeth and growling. They stand staring at one another until the grey wolf rolls over on her back, a sign of submission.² A wolf will rarely hurt another in such family matters, and Nox Gibuu, the wolf mother, welcomes the grey female into her new pack.

A bright ring has formed around the morning sun. The Gitxsan call this gutk'uhloxs; k'uhloxs is the Gitxsan word for the lunar cycle in January. Another bright light shines for this small wolf pack; the wolf mother is bonding[1] with a strong, young male. As they stand eye to eye, his grey fur contrasts against the deep black of hers. They've been nuzzling[2] and spending more time together. Playful and caring, this is a good sign for the new wolf pack. Once the pair have bonded, Nox Gibuu can grow her family.

¹ **Bonding** is to form a close relationship.

² **Nuzzling** means to lean or snuggle against someone to show affection.

A New Pack

This spring is Nox Gibuu's third Lasa 'yanja, the Budding Trees and Blooming Flowers Moon. She has just had her first litter[1] of five pups. The new additions bring the pack's number to ten, and they will need a lot of food to feed the growing family. Her partner is pacing around the den because he wants to hunt prey. Nox Gibuu surveys her pack and selects those who will help with this hunt.

[1] A **litter** is a group of young animals born at the same time to the same mother.

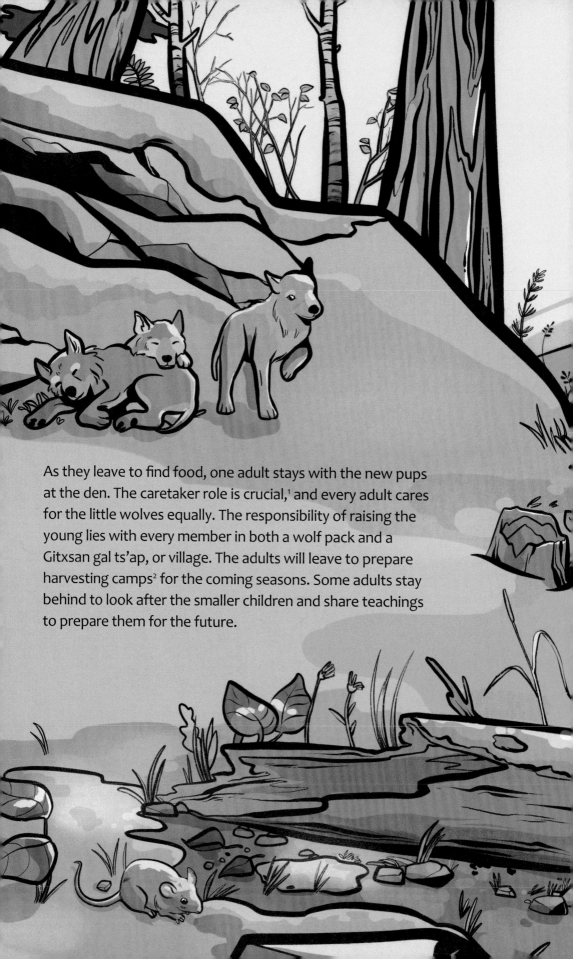

As they leave to find food, one adult stays with the new pups at the den. The caretaker role is crucial,[1] and every adult cares for the little wolves equally. The responsibility of raising the young lies with every member in both a wolf pack and a Gitxsan gal ts'ap, or village. The adults will leave to prepare harvesting camps[2] for the coming seasons. Some adults stay behind to look after the smaller children and share teachings to prepare them for the future.

¹ **Predators** hunt other animals for food.

² A **howl** is a loud and long sound that wolves sing to communicate.

Despite the fear many people have of predators,[1] wolves are some of the most loving and caring beings. They connect through grooming, playful fighting, and sleeping together to stay warm. They also sing songs that travel across the land. Nox Gibuu regularly howls[2] for her little pups. While her howl comforts her family, her music warns any other wolves nearby that this territory belongs to her pack.

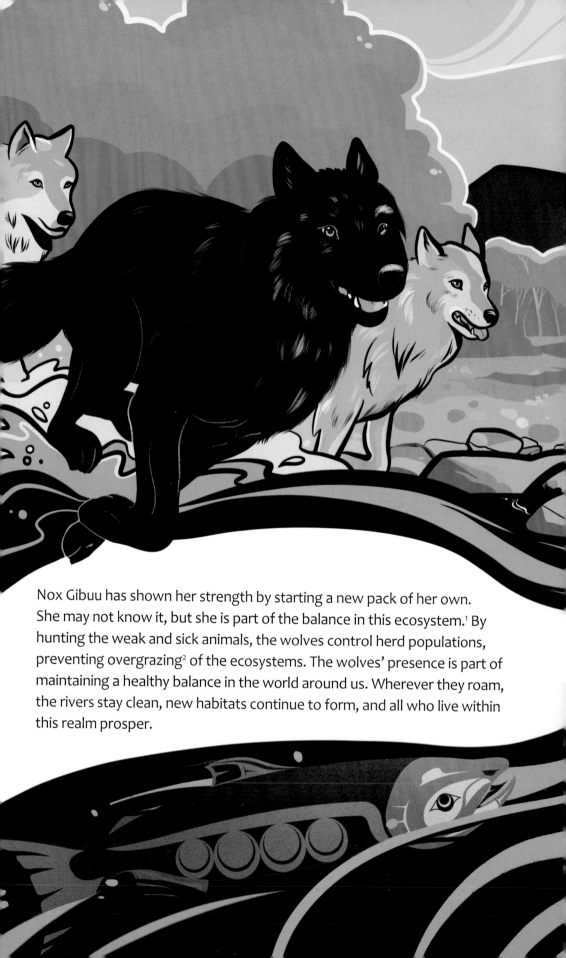

Nox Gibuu has shown her strength by starting a new pack of her own. She may not know it, but she is part of the balance in this ecosystem.[1] By hunting the weak and sick animals, the wolves control herd populations, preventing overgrazing[2] of the ecosystems. The wolves' presence is part of maintaining a healthy balance in the world around us. Wherever they roam, the rivers stay clean, new habitats continue to form, and all who live within this realm prosper.

¹ An **ecosystem** refers to all of the organisms that live within and interact with a specific environment.

² **Overgrazing** is when grazers keep eating without giving plants time to grow.

The Gitxsan

The Gitxsan Nation are Indigenous peoples from their unceded territories of the Northwest Interior of British Columbia. This 35,000 square kilometres of land cradles the headwaters of Xsan or "the River of Mist," also known by its colonial name, the Skeena River. The land defines who they are.

The Nation follows a matrilineal line, and all rights, privileges, names, and stories come from the mothers. The Lax Seel (Frog), Lax Gibuu (Wolf), Lax Skiik (Eagle), and Gisghaast (Fireweed) are the four clans of the people. It is taboo to marry a fellow clan member, even when there are no blood ties.

The four clans are divided among the territories by way of the Wilp system. A Wilp, or "house group," is a group comprising one or more families. Each Wilp has a head chief and wing chiefs, who are guided by Elders and members of their Wilp. Currently, there are 62 house groups, and each governs their portion of the Gitxsan Territories.

The Gitxsan Moons

K'uholxs	Stories and Feasting Moon	January
Lasa hu'mal	Cracking Cottonwood and Opening Trails Moon	February
Wihlaxs	Black Bear's Walking Moon	March
Lasa ya'a	Spring Salmon's Returning Home Moon	April
Lasa 'yanja	Budding Trees and Blooming Flowers Moon	May
Lasa maa'y	Gathering and Preparing Berries Moon	June
Lasa 'wiihun	Fisherman's Moon	July
Lasa lik'i'nxsw	Grizzly Bear's Moon	August
Lasa gangwiikw	Groundhog Hunting Moon	September
Lasa xsin laaxw	Catching-Lots-of-Trout Moon	October
Lasa gwineekxw	Getting-Used-to-Cold Moon	November
Lasa 'wiigwineekxw or Lasa gunkw' ats	Severe Snowstorms and Sharp Cold Moon	December
Ax wa	Shaman's Moon	a blue moon, which is a second full moon in a single month

Stekyodin

Bulkley River

Skeena River

Kispiox River